Max Can Do It!

Written by Charlotte Raby

Illustrated by Sam Hearn

Collins

Bee Rex had fun dashing about.
She had fun crashing in the trees.

Max Rex was not like his sister.
He was not big.
He had fun looking at things.

Bee Rex had fun swinging in the trees.
She was quick!

Max said, "I cannot do that.
I am not quick."
He had fun plodding and squelching
in the mud.

Bee Rex had fun shouting and hunting.

Max said, "I cannot do that.
I am not loud."
He had fun looking at bugs under rocks.

Max went to swim in a deep pool. Then ...

Crash! Smash!
Max sprang up and out of the pool.

Bee had got stuck up a tall tree.
"I am tied up. Help me, Max!"
she said.

Max looked up at Bee.
"I *can* do that," he said.

He got help. Soon they had
a ladder.
"Grab the ladder, Bee!" said Max.

Max got Bee back to the ground.
"I cannot do that, Max!" said Bee.

Bee can do it

Max can do it

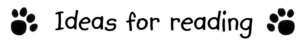 Ideas for reading

Written by Clare Dowdall PhD
Lecturer and Primary Literacy Consultant

Learning objectives: read a range of familiar and common words and simple sentences independently; attempt to read more complex words using phonic knowledge; extend their vocabulary, exploring the meanings and sounds of new words; retell narratives in the correct sequence, drawing on the language patterns of stories; show an understanding of the elements of stories, such as main character, sequence of events, and openings

Curriculum links: Personal, Social and Emotional Development: Making relationships; Self-confidence and self-esteem

Focus phonemes: x, ee, sh, oo, ng

Fast words: was, she, said, they, to

Word count: 162

Getting started

- Look at the front cover and read the title. Discuss who Max is and what might happen in the story.

- Revise the focus phonemes. Write the words that use these phonemes and mark the vowel digraphs with a sound line.

- Focus on the phoneme *x*. Ask children to suggest other words with the *x* phoneme, e.g. box, six, X-ray.

- Using flash cards, look at the fast words. Divide the words into two piles: familiar and unfamiliar. Sound talk the unfamiliar words and discuss the tricky parts of each word, e.g. where the *a* sounds different in *was*.

Reading and responding

- Ask the children to read the book from the beginning aloud, using their phonics skills to sound out each word. Remind them that there will be lots of familiar fast words.

- Move around the group, praising blending and accurate sounding out of new and tricky words with focus phonemes.